MAKE IT

50 Myths and Truths About Creating

Brendan Leonard

Semi-Rad Media

Introduction

I made this book because everyone who has a creative bone in their body can come up with a dozen reasons to not make art. I do it all the time: It probably won't be very good, I'm scared of how I'll feel if people don't like it or if not enough people like it, it's probably just a waste of time that I could be spending doing something "constructive." Maybe you know what I mean?

I've read lots of great books about creating, written by people who are way more successful than me. Every time I read one of those books, I feel inspired. And the next time I sit down at my desk to write or draw or edit video, the inspiration I felt is nowhere to be found—or there isn't enough of it left to power me through writing the first sentence, or putting my marker to paper. It's easier to click over to my email tab and attack my overflowing inbox.

I have fought my way through several hundred days that start just like that, and most days, I don't need more inspiration. I need some tough love, somebody to talk some shit to me to get me started. And that somebody is: me. I have learned to shoot down all my reasons and excuses and just start making the damn thing. Some days I'm quicker at it than other days, but I generally get it done. And I've flexed that muscle enough times that it's almost a reflex now.

I started this project by coming up with a list of questions or assumptions I had at the start of my career, when I had way more rejection letters than bylines, and was working a full-time job during the day but trying to get my writing career started in the evenings. I get paid to do creative work now, and I am grateful for that—but I also get lots of joy out of creating every day, whether it's making up nonsensical song lyrics, writing bad poetry, or creating a recipe from scratch. I love to learn by doing, which means I love to try, then fail, then try again.

I hope one or two of the things in this book help you get started on whatever it is you've always wanted to create, but haven't gotten around to yet.

1

There are no perfect conditions for making art.

READY TO GET STARTED?

CHECKLIST

- □ DOOR CLOSED
- □ COMFORTABLE CHAIR
- □ ROOM TEMPERATURE ACCEPTABLE
- □ GOT ENOUGH SLEEP LAST NIGHT
- □ SILENCE (OR PERFECT MUSIC)
- □ COFFEE OR TEA IS HOT BUT NOT TOO HOT
- □ NOT HUNGRY OR HAVE SNACKS
- □ 100% INSPIRED
- □ WEARING FAVORITE PANTS
- □ FEEL FULFILLED IN ALL OTHER AREAS OF LIFE
- □ NOT ENVIOUS OF ANYONE'S SUCCESS
- □ NO ONE TRYING TO CONTACT ME
- □ NOT WORRIED ABOUT ANYTHING
- □ HAVE PLENTY OF MONEY
- □ USING BEST MATERIALS/EQUIPMENT
- □ EVERYONE LIKES ME
- □ EVERYONE I LOVE WILL LIVE FOREVER
- □ HAVE ZERO UNREAD EMAILS + TEXTS
- □ ALL CAUGHT UP ON NETFLIX + YOUTUBE
- □ HAVE PLENTY OF GROCERIES
- □ OPTIMAL LEVEL OF CREATIVE ANGST

In an interview in the Fall 1969 issue of the *Paris Review*, author E.B. White said, "A writer who waits for ideal conditions under which to work will die without putting a word on paper."

If only you had a cabin in the woods, you'd write that novel you've always wanted to write. If only you could take a few weeks off work and go to that artist's retreat, you'd finally be able to concentrate on your painting without getting distracted by all the other things in your life. Or maybe if you had a beautiful studio with lots of natural light and exposed brick.

Or maybe you just need one more cup of coffee before you get started. Or a different type of music. Or complete silence. Or a glass of wine. Or maybe it's too late in the day, and you should just watch some TV and get up early and work on your story or book or painting or photography tomorrow, when you're fresh.

Or, maybe ... not.

Malik Bendjelloul, whose documentary *Searching for Sugar Man* won an Oscar, ran out of money during production and filmed a few key shots on an iPhone, and finished the film. I'm sure he also put up with all kinds of other hardships that you and I can relate to, like running out of coffee, or not getting exactly eight hours of sleep one or two nights.

2

Giving yourself permission to try is often the biggest obstacle.

PERMISSION SLIP

THIS FORM GUARANTEES _____
(YOUR NAME)

THE RIGHT TO TRY TO MAKE A REAL ART

THING THAT DID NOT EXIST BEFORE, EVEN

IF IT'S NOT THAT GOOD AT FIRST.

_____
(YOUR SIGNATURE)

_____
(DATE)

Here's a sentiment that may be vaguely familiar, or very familiar, or even sound like a certain voice you've had in your head for months or years now:

I'd like to take up painting, or try writing some short stories, or take a pottery class, or [insert any creative way to spend your time] but [insert reason that sounds like something a reasonable adult living in a capitalist society would say]. Or:

- You would love to do some writing, but you haven't written anything since that workshop you took in college, and anyway, who would read it?

- You could pick up your old guitar and noodle on it a little bit this weekend, but you'd feel better if you caught up on some work emails.

- Sure, you'd love to get a new 17-40mm camera lens, but you should really be putting that money in your 401(k) or kid's college fund.

Whatever it is the creative part of you wants to do, it doesn't feel important enough. Maybe because you're sure it won't be good enough, or good at all, and you're an adult—you can't be seen doing things you're not good at, right?

That's certainly one way to live. Another way would be to try things you are curious about, and maybe even really bad at, in order to learn something new. This requires giving yourself permission to try, which is really per-mission to be bad at something, which is humbling, but probably interesting, and if you stick with it, potentially very satisfying. So write yourself a permission slip.

3

There is no good art or bad art.

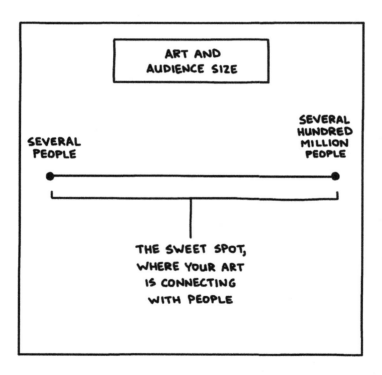

There's art you like, and art you don't like. If you go around telling people Taylor Swift's music is objectively not good, millions of Taylor Swift fans would disagree with you. Does that make her music the best ever created? (That's a rhetorical question—I do not think it's a good use of anyone's time to publicly argue about that point.)

Some art has a very large audience (like Taylor Swift's), and some art has a very small audience. Sometimes your mom is the only person who thinks your crayon drawing is any good. That's OK. Sometimes you write a letter to affect only one person, but if that one person is affected in the right way, maybe you get married to that person. That's success, even if a million people don't think you're a great writer.

Some people, like, say, Vin Diesel, make a piece of art so popular that they can't go to the grocery store to buy an avocado without being recognized and mobbed by crowds of people wanting a selfie with them. Some people make a piece of art that only a dozen people love, but they love it enough that it's worth it for the person who created it.

4

Art is not math—there's no "wrong" way to do it.

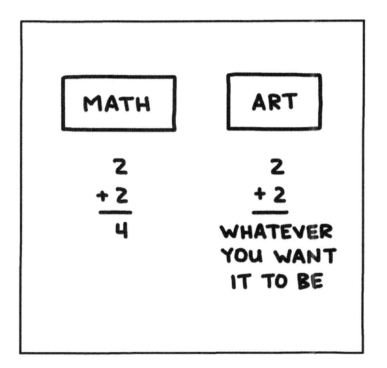

We've all had a wrong answer on a math test at some point in our lives. There's not a lot of wiggle room in basic math—if you divide 400 by 20 and you come up with the answer 2,736, that's incorrect. Which is probably what your math teacher said when you did something wrong on a math assignment in elementary school: This is incorrect.

But do you think anyone listened to Queen's "Bohemian Rhapsody"—arguably a very unconventional rock song—for the first time and said, "No, this is incorrect"? Or stood in front of one of Mark Rothko's canvases in a museum and said to their friend, "This painting is wrong"?

There are no wrong answers in art, and that can be either:

1. quite paralyzing if you're a person who is most motivated by doing things "correctly" and getting a right answer

2. extremely liberating because you can do whatever you want

5

Lucky you, you have everything you need to never be bored again.

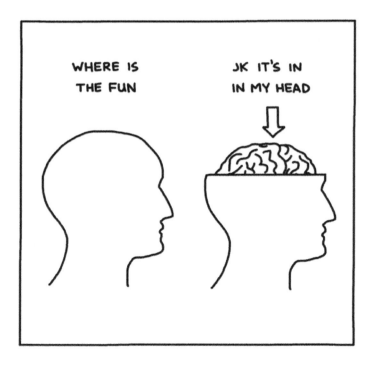

My friend Nick said to me one time that there are two types of people in the world: People who look for fun things to do, and people who make their own fun.

I am always leery of "there are two types of people in the world" statements, but I do think Nick is onto something, in that we all have two ways to spend our spare time: looking for fun things to do, or making our own fun.

Looking for fun things to do is: using our spare time to click around Netflix or YouTube trying to find a new show or movie to watch, buying tickets to a concert, or going to an art gallery. Making our own fun is: taking our camera on a hike to shoot photos of mountains or trees, trying to perfect a pineapple fried rice recipe, or writing a short story.

Both of these are enjoyable ways to spend our time, but making your own fun never has any supply chain issues. You never find yourself saying "There's nothing good on [streaming service X, Y, and/or Z] right now," or "I don't like any of the bands playing in town this month," or "I saw all the stuff at the local galleries already during the art walk last week."

If being creative is your source of fun, you just make something. Even if it's the worst piece of garbage you've ever made, and you feel like it was a total waste of time (it wasn't), at least you weren't bored while you were doing it.

6

Most of the time, it will probably not feel "inspired."

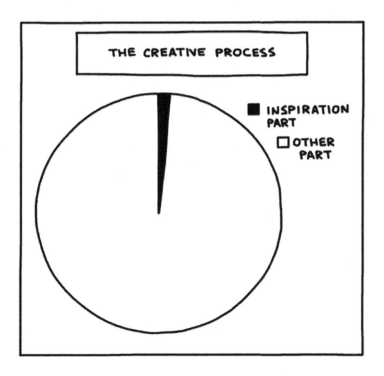

Most of it will feel like work. For every sentence that comes into your head as if placed there by a lightning bolt from the gods of prose, you will have to write 100 others that feel as inspired as shoveling snow out of your driveway so you can drive to work on a Monday morning.

One of my favorite quotes about making art comes from artist Chuck Close, who said, "Inspiration is for amateurs. The rest of us just show up and get to work."

7

It's OK to do something other than art in order to make a living.

THE DREAM	THE REALITY
"IF I WERE A FULL-TIME WRITER, I COULD FOCUS ON MY WRITING ALL DAY, EVERY DAY"	"I FEEL LIKE 90 PERCENT OF MY WRITING CAREER IS WRITING EMAILS"

As great as quitting your job to follow your dreams sounds (and looks on social media), it simply won't work for a lot of people—and it's also not the only way to create art. A "real job" can be a blessing. It takes a certain type of person to want to create full-time, and even when that person decides to do it, half of their "work" time will be spent on non-creative stuff—writing e-mails, making phone calls, scheduling meetings with people, doing all the things necessary to sell their art and make a living at it (so they don't have to work a "real job").

If waiting tables or wrangling spreadsheets pays your rent so you can paint during the hours you're not at work, you're still a "real painter." If wedding photography pays the bills and gives you the freedom to take one trip to Nepal (or even somewhere a couple hundred miles away!) each year to shoot the photos that inspire you, that's winning.

8

You have to believe in your art at least enough to create it.

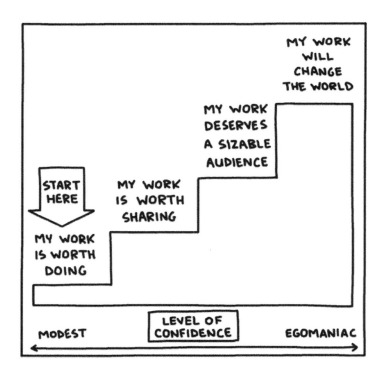

In a 2015 interview on WTF *with Marc Maron*, actor and writer Jason Segel said: "I think that anyone who's a performer is a very unique personality type, in that you believe somewhere that what you have to express artistically is worthy of people paying money for and being quiet and listening to."

Do you think your art is worth something, whether it's thousands of dollars or just the time it would cost someone to experience whatever you're creating? You can answer that question either "yes" or "not quite yet," but you can't answer it "no."

Better question: Could your art thing, whatever it is, potentially make someone's day better in some way? ("Someone" includes you, by the way.)

9

Don't get hung up on a specific medium.

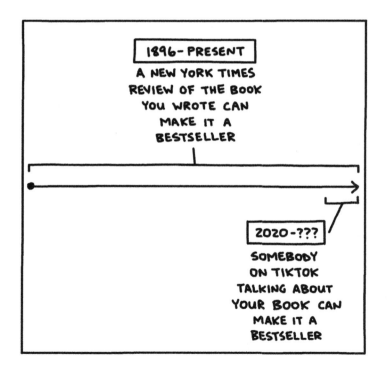

Casey Neistat, who made most of his living on commercial projects before becoming famous as a renegade filmmaker, identifies himself with the somewhat underwhelming title of "YouTuber." Several of his short films have been viewed millions of times, but he holds true to what he spends most of his time doing: recording and editing vlogs for YouTube. He found something he enjoyed, and poured his daily efforts into it, whether it made him money or not. And it eventually did.

We live in an era of media where change is nearly constant. Be open to new (and old) mediums, and don't be afraid to try something out—you might just fall in love with it and find a big audience for your work there (and community, and maybe even some financial reward, if you're into that).

Sure, plenty of photographers would say the ultimate success is getting their writing published in *The New Yorker*, but plenty of writers are finding artistic fulfillment (and even making a living) by self-publishing ebooks, growing a weekly newsletter, and writing mini-essays in Instagram captions or Twitter threads.

10

It's OK to imitate others' work—up to a point.

EAT, PRAY, LOVE

BY
ELIZABETH
GILBERT

MUCH LIKE
ELIZABETH
GILBERT,
I ALSO
TRAVELED TO
ROME, INDIA,
AND BALI

BY ME

Thousands of writers' first efforts no doubt resemble authors we've all read—Hunter S. Thompson, Ernest Hemingway, Sylvia Plath. Certain photography rules exist because they work for everyone, regardless of style. Understanding why something is good is a great place to start creating—and imitating something generally regarded as high quality is certainly way more likely to be successful than imitating something that no one likes. We've all heard great covers of popular songs, and we've all been subjected to, uh, not-as-great karaoke versions of popular songs.

Using your own experiences, knowledge, and personality to develop and express your own style, whatever it is, will result in something more original and authentic, will likely be more fun and fulfilling, and will probably help you reach more people. Think about it this way: If you wanted to watch a Wes Anderson movie, wouldn't you just watch a Wes Anderson movie, not an imitation of a Wes Anderson movie?

11

Make gifts for your friends.

Your friends are your first and best audience, and your window to understand what other people will like when it comes to art.

Instead of worrying about the "quality" of a story, or the technical aspects of a photo or painting, imagine what you want people to get out of what you're creating. Think of the people most familiar to you when you start to build your idea, rather than "the world." The world is a huge audience with lots of wildly differing needs—some people just want to watch action movies, but other people don't mind a good emotionally open story. You may be able to reach both, but it's probably better to concentrate on one group and start there. And your friends, or people who at least think somewhat like you, are a great place to start.

Why are you making the art you're making? If you create a painting that communicates something about your past or ongoing body image issues, and if it helps other people understand or deal with their own similar struggles, isn't that a positive impact on someone else's life? If you write a song about heartbreak and other people who have had their hearts broken can relate to it, isn't that a form of success?

In his 2009 YouTube video, *The Gift of Gary Busey*, bestselling author John Green dispensed this advice to people who asked him how to become a writer:

"Don't make stuff because you want to make money—it will never make you enough money. And don't make stuff because you want to get famous—because you will never feel famous enough. Make gifts for people—and work hard on making those gifts in the hope that those people will notice and like the gifts. Maybe they will notice how hard you worked, and maybe they won't—and if they don't notice, I know it's frustrating. But, ultimately, that doesn't change anything—because your responsibility is not to the people you're making the gift for, but to the gift itself."

12

Giving it away for free can be a form of marketing.

Getting your work in front of an audience always costs something, whether it's money you pay to advertise it, or time you spend making it "for free."

You might tell yourself, "I'm a [writer/photographer/singer]; I'm not doing this for free," and wait until you can sell your song or photos or story. Or, you might take whatever chance you get to share your art (open mics, selling art at farmer's markets, writing for low-paying publications, etc.) in hopes that the appropriate monetary compensation will come later.

Pop art icon Keith Haring didn't just explode onto the early 1980s New York art scene at the beginning—he painted his unmistakable crawling babies and other designs on blank spaces reserved for ads in New York's subways. Nobody paid him to do that, but it essentially functioned as a citywide advertising campaign for his brand and his art.

Haring understood that graffiti (although, yes, technically illegal) was the best way to get his work in front of eight million people. So he gave it away, and it didn't cost him anything but paint (and the risk of being arrested). No matter the medium, word-of-mouth will always be the best advertising.

Fast-forward a few decades, and thousands of creators have discovered that they can write short jokes on Twitter, or post photos and captions on Instagram, or create videos for YouTube and TikTok—while not getting paid at all, just like Keith Haring's graffiti—but in a relatively short time, maybe get noticed by a few people, and maybe even begin to get paid for their work.

Social media companies, of course, love for you to pay them to "boost" the exposure of your work, and other companies love to ask artists to use their creative work in exchange for "exposure" to the brand's large audience. Can these tactics work? Sure. Lots of artists hate these practices, as they feel they're just a way companies take advantage of creatives (which can also be true). If you find yourself in that position, you'll have to decide.

13

Creativity can cost nothing but your time, and that time can be the time of your life.

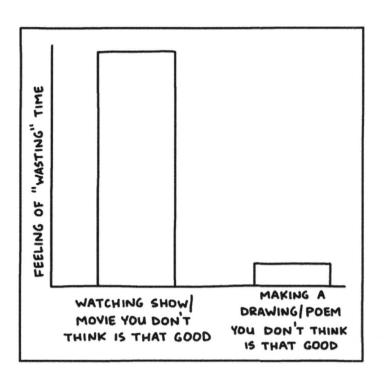

If you're not creating, your free time can become an endless search for something to distract you: a new movie to watch, a new game to play, a new show to binge-watch on Netflix, bouncing from one social media app to the next and back again looking for anything that will entertain you for a few minutes. Or, for probably very little or no money, you can create something.

A famous rapper once said, "You're never poor when you're doing something creative." Buying and renting things to entertain you costs money. Making creative things can be free (or very inexpensive). The musicians who created the first hip hop songs in the early 1970s started with no musical instruments besides turntables—which were up until that point devices for listening to recorded music, not making new music. Plenty of artists have begun learning their craft starting with a pad and pencil, or painting on walls, or taking photos with a phone.

14

You're only a "starving artist" if you're actually making art.

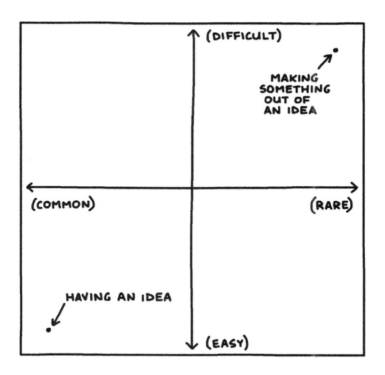

If every day after you get off work, you're sitting in a bar telling someone about the book you'd like to write someday, you're note making much progress on that book.

You don't necessarily have to have a monastic devotion to your art (although that might be a productive strategy), but don't bullshit yourself. There are a million people who would love to create something "someday," but for whatever reason(s), they never even take the first step.

To paraphrase many writers and creatives: The idea is the easy part. It takes little mental or physical effort to have a dream, especially if you perpetually procrastinate the actual work it would take to realize that dream. Making something, on the other hand, and having the courage to put it out there, will require hours of trying, fucking up, re-doing, worrying if it's good enough or true enough or exactly what you wanted to say in the first place, and more hours of trying, before you nervously send it out to whatever audience you believe needs it. And all that stuff is the scary part, which is why all those big ideas never get started in the first place and die at the bottom of a beer glass or under a pile of other stuff we think is "more important."

Hopefully you believe in yourself enough to at least try. Every starving artist who tries does so with at least some belief that one day, they won't starve as much to make their art, even if their paintings only sell for enough money to fund buying more canvases or brushes and keep their creative life going. As filmmaker and surf photographer Mickey Smith said in the film *Dark Side of the Lens*, "If I only scrape a living, at least it's a living worth scraping."

15

Start with what you know.

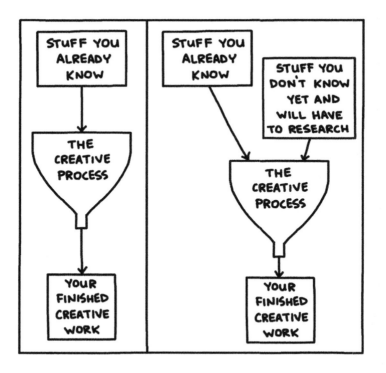

The classic advice to beginning writers says to "write what you know," because it's the most believable. Obviously science fiction writers have ignored this for decades and had great success. I believe the advice should be "start with what you know," or the stories closest to your heart, or even closest to your house. You can learn the basics of a craft trying something familiar—writing personal stories or a memoir, painting landscapes of scenes near where you live, writing songs about the things closest to your heart. You already know the language of familiar things, so start there.

Once you've acquired mastery of the elements of telling the "story" of something easier, branch out from there. Depicting something you have less knowledge of requires research, and that's an extra step (and sometimes the biggest step) in addition to knowing how to set a scene, or where to point a camera.

Nas's 1994 album *Illmatic* is almost universally hailed as one of the greatest hip hop albums of all time (if not the greatest), and its subject matter barely covers anything outside New York City, and for the most part only the Queensbridge housing projects, where Nas grew up. It was what he knew, and his vision of life there was more vivid and intriguing than any other artist had ever communicated. Talking about his neighborhood, in the best way he knew how, vaulted him to stardom—and after that, of course, he traveled the world. But first, he wrote about what he knew best.

16

Don't take criticism personally.

Especially on social media. As we all know, many people believe their opinion is the most important thing they can contribute to the world, and—this may come as a surprise—sometimes they don't consider anyone else when they're typing out their current thoughts. If your art reaches a big enough audience, someone like this will probably find you. It's pretty easy to let one person's off-the-cuff remark get to you, even if it's the only one out of a hundred comments, or a thousand. People will tell you to develop a "thick skin," and maybe you will, eventually—or rather, you'll learn to dismiss (or at least ignore) criticism that has no constructive purpose.

Obviously there's a place for well-thought-out, informed criticism. If your film or book is being reviewed in the *New York Times*, you're aware of this (and you're probably not reading this book). But if you find yourself getting depressed because of a two-star Amazon.com review of your book, written by someone whose only other reviews are a toaster oven and an anti-itch ointment that didn't work, remember how easy it is for anyone to criticize your artistic effort versus how hard it is to work up the courage to put something out there.

In the movie *Birdman*, when first-time director Riggan Thomas confronts theater critic Tabitha Dickinson in a bar, she says she is going to "destroy" his play in her review, even though she hasn't seen it yet. Thomas, at the end of a brief diatribe, says, "You write a couple of paragraphs and you know what ... none of this costs you fucking anything. You risk nothing. Nothing. Nothing. Nothing. Well I'm a fucking actor. This play cost me everything."

17

It's OK to fake it until you make it (with some humility).

You don't grow without taking risks, and at some point, hopefully someone will find your work, and say, "I liked what I saw of your last project. Could you do something like that, but way bigger, for me?" And you have two choices: You can take the safe route and say no, or you can say yes and maybe lose some sleep worrying if you're good enough and if they will actually like what you come up with. And that's one way to push yourself to improve: external motivation. If you wait until you're ready, you'll never be ready. No one is ever ready. If you're ready for whatever it is, whatever it is will be boring the entire time you're working on it.

18

If you want people to see your work, you will have to put it out there.

To paraphrase a musician I knew once: The greatest guitar player in the entire world, whoever you think that is, left their basement practice space and stood up on a stage to share it at some point. Otherwise you'd never have heard what they were capable of, and they would only be the greatest guitar player in their entire basement. And they were probably a bit nervous when they finally did leave their basement.

19

Putting your work out there doesn't mean anyone's going to read/watch/listen to it.

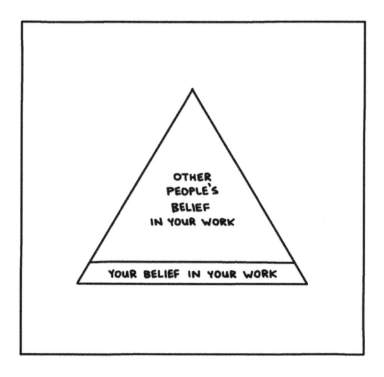

Maybe you've said this to yourself, or to a friend: "I'm just not comfortable promoting myself."

That's OK, and probably more than OK, as it is a good sign you're not a narcissist. Or at least not a huge narcissist. But if you want people to actually see your work, you might have to give yourself a little pep talk about self-promotion. You worked hard on that thing, whatever it is—at least hard enough to tell a few people about it, right? Great.

You'll probably have to tell them three or four times. Don't apologize about that. The world is a busy, distracting place, and no matter where you put your writing, photos, art, or films, the easiest thing for people to do is ignore it. But if you want people to come to your birthday party, you have to tell them about your birthday party. And it's the same with promoting your art. Everyone has a different comfort level with it—some musicians don't mind playing their guitar in subway stations with a hat sitting at their feet for donations; some writers are terrified of reading their work at book signings.

The fairy tale of someone being "discovered" out of nowhere is rare. If you have ever enjoyed a piece of art, it's because at some point, whoever created it believed in it enough to get it in front of you, whether it's a song, a book, a painting, or a film. You don't have to "sell" people on it, or be arrogant, or overhype it (although those things have worked for more than one person)—you just have to believe in it enough to ask people to give it a chance. Remember, at one point in history, somebody in southern Italy invented pizza, and said to someone else, "Hey, I made this, and I think it tastes OK—wanna try it?" And that ended up being a pretty good deal for everyone.

20

Making something will always be better than wondering if you could do it.

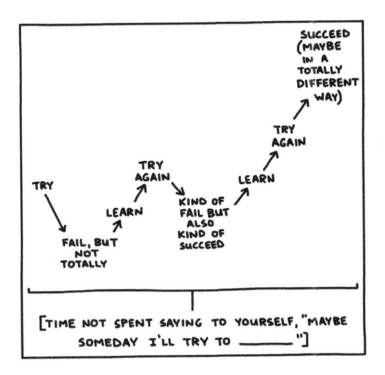

Thousands of people have committed themselves to National Novel Writing Month and hammered out 2,000 words per day to complete a rough draft of a book. Lots of those books have never been published, but all those people stepped up to the plate and found out they could do it, instead of daydreaming about it. Maybe that first 60,000-word effort resulted in a great first draft of a book, or taught them that they should never try to write another book, but more likely, it taught them a lot of things they could do next time, and gave them the confidence to try it again—maybe giving themselves more than a month to write a first draft.

So try, and see what happens. You never know—you might look back on all that time you spent trying, and remember it as the best part.

21

If you make a lot of art, you might always hate the stuff you did five years ago.

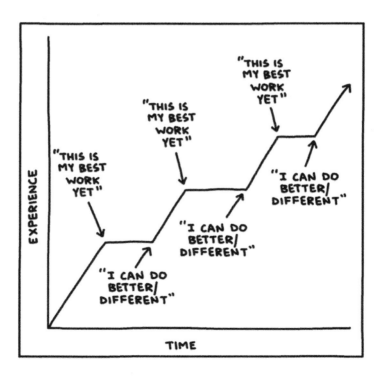

No matter who you are, if you keep at it, you will always be a better painter/photographer/musician/writer than you were yesterday. And reading what you wrote a year or two ago will probably be horrifying. Don't judge yourself too harshly, because someone probably loved your two-year-old work. Let them judge it. Dave Eggers in 2007 told Debbie Millman of *Design Matters* that he hated his book A *Heartbreaking Work of Staggering Genius*, published in 2000. But thousands of other people loved it—it was a No. 1 *New York Times* bestseller and a Pulitzer Prize finalist.

If you are making art, and continually trying to improve, of course you're going to look back and feel like your older stuff is not as good. That's a positive thing—hopefully it means you're getting better at what you do. It doesn't mean any of that stuff is bad, either (hey, Dave Eggers, I loved A *Heartbreaking Work of Staggering Genius* when I read it in 2001!). It just means you've moved on, in a different, probably upward, direction.

22

You might suck at first.

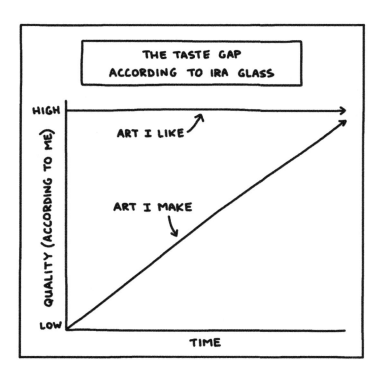

THE TASTE GAP
ACCORDING TO IRA GLASS

QUALITY (ACCORDING TO ME)

HIGH

LOW

ART I LIKE

ART I MAKE

TIME

Most people suck at first. It's a fact. True prodigies are rare in any pursuit. Even a first-time author whose book lands on the bestseller list wrote dozens of thousands of words before that one book was published. It's easy to feel entitled to success because you've tried really hard on your first efforts, but that's a pretty high expectation to put on yourself. Give yourself some grace, and some time to try things out, and see what works and what doesn't.

In an interview with Current TV years ago, *This American Life* creator Ira Glass shared some now very famous thoughts on why we all think our first efforts are terrible:

"Nobody tells this to people who are beginners—I wish someone told me. All of us who do creative work, we get into it because we have good taste. But there is this gap. For the first couple years you make stuff, it's just not that good. It's trying to be good, it has potential, but it's not. But your taste, the thing that got you into the game, is still killer. And your taste is why your work disappoints you. A lot of people never get past this phase, they quit. Most people I know who do interesting, creative work went through years of this. We know our work doesn't have this special thing that we want it to have. We all go through this. And if you are just starting out or you are still in this phase, you gotta know its normal and the most important thing you can do is do a lot of work. ... It's gonna take a while. It's normal to take a while. You've just gotta fight your way through."

23

Don't do it for the money.

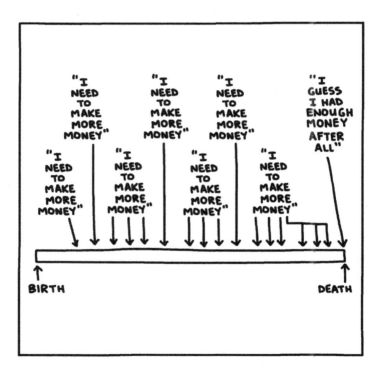

It can be easy to daydream about selling a bajillion books, or getting rich and famous off your music, or getting famous and then rich, as if your art could be a sort of winning lottery ticket.

But there's a reason people's parents want them to grow up to have well-paying, secure jobs, not become writers and musicians and painters. Creative things don't make very many people rich, at least in the financial sense. It's probably not a good idea to treat creative work like a part-time job, where you divide the amount of money you make by the hours you put into it, and then use that metric to decide if it's "worth it."

If you're not one of the top, say, 300 musical acts in the world, is it worth it? It's up to you. Is success making $50,000 a year to play music, or making $50,000 a year to write books and magazine articles? If it is, you can do it and be rich—or at least "rich." But if your primary goal is making a million dollars, you may have to adjust your expectations at some point.

Pearl Jam didn't decide to become a band and make music because they wanted to be rich and famous (although they did do both those things). After 30-plus years, do you think they still play together because they still feel some need to get richer and more famous? Obviously only they can answer that on a personal level, but I'd bet they're still doing it because they still enjoy it in some way.

If you approach making art with the idea that any money you make is a bonus, on top of the enjoyment you already get from making and sharing the art, it will feel less like a job—and probably result in better art.

24

Your next great piece of art is probably not going to come out of a glowing screen.

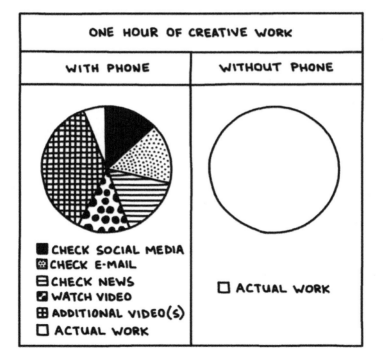

Do you need one more person to tell you to put down your phone? Here's something my friend Forest said to me that I think about all the time:

"No one likes to see someone they respect staring at a phone."

Phones and tablets are great for a lot of things, but unless you're actively creating something one them, you're probably just sitting there like a zombie breathing through your mouth hoping that screen will bring up something that will entertain you for the next 20 to 2,000 seconds, and a few political articles, comment threads, memes, and cat videos later, suddenly you've lost an hour of time you could have spent making something. I know this because I've done it a million times.

Scrolling is procrastinating. You need stillness in order for your mind to create, so put down your phone, close your laptop, go for a walk, and when you come back, start making whatever it is you want to make.

25

Nobody is going to magically bestow the title "artist" on you someday.

Or "writer," or photographer, or musician, or filmmaker, or sculptor, or dancer, or actor. If you do enough of it, you'll start to feel like it fits.

Do you have to do it for a living in order to say "I'm an artist"? Good question. Here's another question about titles: If I said, "My dad's a golfer," would you think he gets paid to golf? I mean, he wouldn't turn it down, but sadly, no, he does not get paid to golf. But based on the amount of time he spends golfing, he's a golfer.

For some reason, though, it can feel a little weird calling yourself a writer, or an artist, or a photographer. Maybe that's because we think people might expect big things out of us, or assume we have some level of talent, or notoriety, when we say, "I'm an artist."

It doesn't matter if other people think you're an artist, or if you ever say "I'm an artist" out loud. What matters is doing it enough to feel like it's a part of who you are. The important thing is to stop saying, "I want to be a _____ someday," and to start making things.

26

You are going to get rejected.

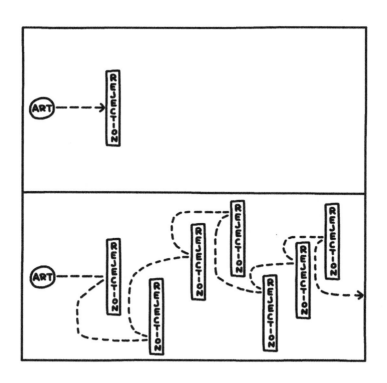

It's usually not you. You never know what that editor or casting director or gallery owner is thinking, or looking for. Sometimes it's a reason that makes no sense—maybe the magazine already ran another story about the desert this year and they have an unwritten quota of only one desert story per year, or maybe the casting director doesn't like dark-haired actors because of an unfortunate dating experience in college, or maybe they burned their toast that morning before your audition, or maybe five minutes after your pitch e-mail was sent they accidentally deleted their entire e-mail inbox.

But sometimes it is you. Maybe you don't really understand that literary journal's audience or needs as well as you think you do, or maybe you didn't nail the reading because you didn't 100 percent identify with the role, or maybe your paintings are a little too, say, abstract for the people who usually buy art from that particular gallery. Maybe your stuff isn't ready yet, even though you think it is, but in six months, it will be. Maybe that magazine will reject your story idea and you'll pitch it somewhere else a month later and see that, yes, it's a much better fit at the second magazine.

But sometimes it's not you. Sometimes people suck at answering e-mail. Sometimes they reject you because they're having a bad day and you happened to pitch them on the exact wrong day, lucky you. Sometimes people in gatekeeper positions don't know shit about good art, and they're only the editor or casting director because they're someone's brother-in-law. Sometimes people make terrible decisions for no reason (like that person who cut you off on the freeway last Wednesday). You will never know.

Keep trying. A hundred bestsellers got rejected by a hundred publishers each before they landed at the exact perfect place, and maybe then some of those 99 publishers said, "Well, we really blew it on that one." But that author kept trying, and because they did, thousands of people got to read a really good story.

27

You will doubt yourself. Pretty much everyone doubts themselves.

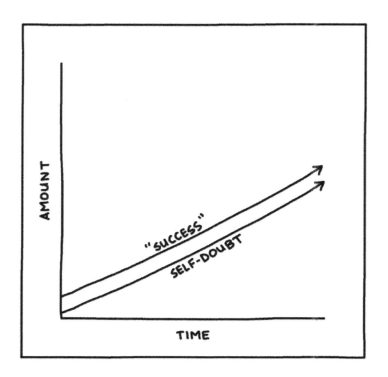

Every creative (and probably everyone else doing anything that challenges them) experiences what's known as Impostor Syndrome—the phenomenon psychologists Pauline Clance and Suzanne Imes defined in the journal *Psychotherapy: Theory, Research and Practice* in 1978 as the feeling of "phoniness in people who believe that they are not intelligent, capable or creative despite evidence of high achievement."

So you're not the only one who's not sure you have what it takes—even author Maya Angelou has famously admitted a nagging fear that someone is going to come out of nowhere and revoke her "writer" title someday. Or, as bestselling author David Foster Wallace put it in the interviews that became the film *The End of the Tour*, "The more people think you're great, the bigger the fear of being a fraud is."

28

If you're making art and sharing it, every day is a day something great can happen.

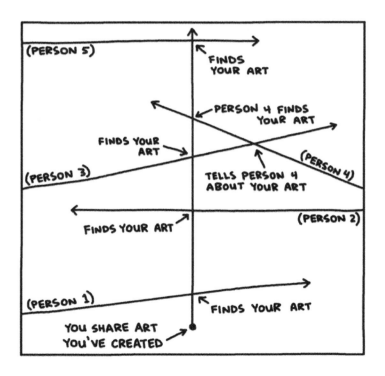

Have you ever been in a bookstore or library and found a book that was published 20 or 30 years ago, read it, and thought something along the lines of, "Wow, that was great. I'm so glad that person made that book"? Or watched a classic movie? Or discovered someone's four-year-old YouTube video of their acoustic cover of a song, and loved it so much you played it 10 or 15 times throughout the rest of the day?

One of the great things about making creative work is that it provides joy, and/or meaning, and/or solace to people long after it's left your hands to go out into the world. Any day, someone might reach out to you and tell you how much something you made meant to them, or just to say they're a fan, or to say they're a fan and ask if you'd maybe like to collaborate on something sometime? Your work is out there in the world doing things you may never hear about—hopefully positive things. And if they come back to you in some way, hopefully you appreciate them (I call these types of things "emotional paychecks," as they may not pay my electric bill, but they keep me motivated to keep making art).

29

Nobody makes art all by themselves.

As much as we love the narrative of the lone creative toiling away at their craft until they've built the most brilliant album or book or painting the world has ever seen, that's not the truth almost 100 percent of the time.

Yes, making art requires a ton of effort, and lots of that effort is by the artist themselves (sometimes nearly all of the effort), but going it alone is not a great strategy for good work or great mental health. Reach out to friends to give your story a quick read, or their opinion on a joke you're writing, or their feedback on a video edit, or just to give you some tough love in the form of telling you to stop complaining and keep at it. There's a reason Grammy and Oscar acceptance speeches are lists of people's names, and why the acknowledgements section of a book is sometimes a couple pages long.

30

Don't think you need someone to take care of your basic needs so you can focus on your art.

When I was in college, a successful full-time freelance writer told my magazine writing class the popular myth that "If you want to be a freelance writer, you need a trust fund or an understanding spouse with a good job."

Either of those things would obviously be quite helpful, but that statement is of course not always true. After taking that class, I worked full-time non-writing jobs for six years, writing in my spare time, before I had enough freelance work to quit my 40-hour-a-week job to pursue writing full-time. I'm not unique in doing that—other, much more successful creatives have produced great things while holding down a "real job" and working on their art in the margins of their days.

Like Toni Morrison, who was not only working full-time as a book editor at Random House, but was a single mother to two young sons when she wrote *The Bluest Eye*, getting up at 4 a.m. every day to work on it.

Having a day job takes up a huge chunk of time and brainpower, and we all have lots of other obligations in our lives. But you have to ask yourself: Are those really the things preventing you from making art? I don't know everything about Toni Morrison, but I can guarantee she wasn't spending any of her spare time on Twitter or TikTok when she wrote *The Bluest Eye*, because the book came out in 1970.

31

At some point, you might have to say yes to something that terrifies you.

It's scary to put your work out there, and it can be even scarier when your worst fears are realized—and someone actually likes it. Even worse, people might offer to pay you for your work (also scary—it can't be worth that much money, can it?). And the absolutely most terrifying: When someone likes your work enough that they ask if you'd be interested in doing something a bit outside of your current comfort zone? You're like, "What happened? Just yesterday I was playing the guitar in my basement! How could anyone think I was qualified for [something outside of my basement]? That's crazy!"

But it happens. You might be presented with opportunities that scare you, and you'll have to decide to say yes or no. There's nothing wrong with saying no to something (not every opportunity is a good fit), but you have to decide if you're saying no because it's a bad fit, or because of fear.

In a 2014 commencement speech at Maharishi University, Jim Carrey said:

"So many of us choose our path out of fear disguised as practicality. What we really want seems impossibly out of reach and ridiculous to expect, so we never dare to ask the universe for it. My father could have been a great comedian, but he didn't believe that was possible for him, and so he made a conservative choice. Instead, he got a safe job as an accountant, and when I was 12 years old, he was let go from that safe job and our family had to do whatever we could to survive.

I learned many great lessons from my father, not the least of which was that you can fail at what you don't want, so you might as well take a chance on doing what you love."

32

You don't need anyone else's approval, or money, to do it.

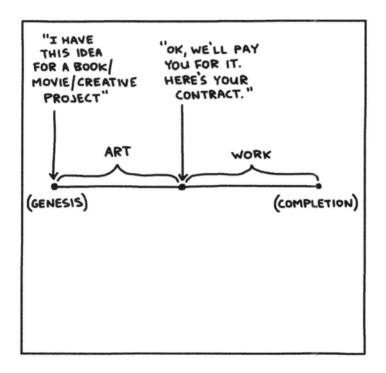

A writer friend once told me that it was her goal to have a book published in two years. I said she should absolutely do it, and that it only cost me about $100 to self-publish my first book. She said she had difficulty making time to work on a (theoretically) non-paying project like a book, and that she had thought about starting a crowdfunding campaign to finance it. I told her that if she really believed in the book, she would just write it, and not try to get paid for it before she'd even started the writing process (although she was right—getting paid while you're doing it would be nice).

Art that you produce without a paycheck is 100 percent inspiration and drive, and although most writers, photographers, and filmmakers might hesitate to admit it, once someone is paying you for your art, it can start to feel a little bit like work—and the inspiration to create is somewhat compromised. Once you owe it to someone else, the book (or short film or photo essay or art installation), becomes something you have to do, and maybe less something you want to do.

To start a project just because you want to create it is to harness that fire that makes you want to create in the first place. It stays pure, because the only stakeholders in the artistic process are you and the audience you imagine seeing (and hopefully loving) the finished product. No one changes the direction of your vision, and more importantly, no one can reject the project or tell you it's a terrible idea while you're working on it.

Fifty years ago, to write a story and get it in front of an audience, you had to submit it to a magazine or a newspaper or a publisher. To make a song or a movie, you had to go through a record label or studio. There are far fewer barriers to entry these days: Filmmakers can make and edit short movies on phones, writers can start free blogs, and photographers can take photos and share them with people immediately. No one can reject your dream, and no one can keep you from putting it out there.

33

It's not the camera. Or the notebook.

Any professional photographer can probably tell you a story about someone who saw their work somewhere and said to them, "You must have a really nice camera." Which of course is a bit of an insult to that photographer's skill, hard work, and knowledge of photography concepts. If a nice camera was all you needed to take great photos, anybody with $5,000 to spare could buy an expensive camera and blow us all away. But they don't.

Tools can make a difference, or course, but they won't ever do the work for you. I have to remind myself of this every time I am about to buy myself yet another fancy notebook (surely this will be the one!).

A fairly well-known story about Jay-Z: Before he was Jay-Z, he was Shawn Carter, a guy who at times made a living selling crack. While standing on street corners, he would come up with rap lyrics in his head, and lacking a notebook to write them down, would run into a bodega and buy something just so he could have a paper bag to scrawl the verses on before he forgot them. Sometimes, he wouldn't be near a bodega, so he'd just memorize the lyrics, which led to his legendary practice of going into the studio with nothing written down, and rapping off the top of his head.

34

There is no single path to success.

Yes, getting a story published in the *New Yorker* is a measure of success. So is recording an album that goes platinum, or writing a bestselling book. But they're not the only measures. And you shouldn't have tunnel vision on what you consider success, especially in this age of ever-evolving media. Photographer Chris Burkard has never* had a photo printed on the cover of *National Geographic*. But do you think he worries about that? Four million people see his photos on Instagram every day.

By the time you get whatever it is you think is the true mark of success, that type of media may be extinct, or on its way out. Or, your idea of what you really want may have changed. Marc Maron was in the midst of a lull in his career as a standup comedian interviewing people in his suburban L.A. garage was his last shot at show business success in September 2009. Less than six years later, Maron interviewed the President of the United States in that same garage for his WTF podcast.

It is entirely possible that by the time you read this Chris Burkard will have had one of his photos printed on the cover of National Geographic.

35

When someone else's art succeeds, it doesn't diminish yours.

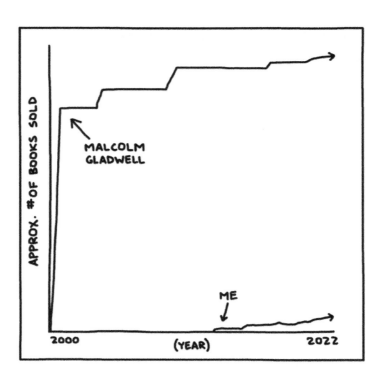

Someone out there is always going to be more successful than you, have more fans than you, more likes than you, more recognition than you, and more awards than you. Hating on them or their work isn't going to make your art any better; it's just making you look like a bitter asshole—which is because you're acting like a bitter asshole. And that's a huge waste of your life.

If what you're doing is interesting at all, you're not doing the exact same thing as anyone else. It's not a tennis match in which you're trying to outscore someone else on a point system. If competition helps drive you to create something better than you might have otherwise, that's great. But wouldn't it be a bummer to not enjoy a song or photo or short film because you see the person who made it as your competition?

36

There is no such thing as "having too much time on your hands."

Sometimes, when a person sees another person doing something they deem foolish, they comment something like "they have too much time on our hands." They forget that we're all privileged to have any spare time on our hands at all, something that was an unforeseeable luxury not too many generations ago, when we spent all of our time trying to survive.

The advance of civilization has given many people the opportunity to have some spare time, and with that spare time, we have found ways to express ourselves. Art, whether it's Shakespeare or Frida Kahlo or *To Pimp a Butterfly* or *Stranger Things*, is created by people with spare time, and consumed by other people with spare time. Some of it we embrace, some of it we discard, and all of it, in the grand scheme of things, is arguably folly.

Charlie Todd, the founder of prank collective Improv Everywhere, once pointed out that hundreds of thousands of people get together in football stadiums on Saturdays and Sundays every fall to watch teams play games—and no one ever says, "those people have too much time on their hands."

Know who else had extra time on their hands? All those athletes we love to watch do amazing things. As a young man, LeBron James, thankfully, didn't say to himself, "You know what I should do with this spare time I have after class? I should get one or more part-time jobs so I'm a more productive member of society." He played basketball instead. And that worked out pretty well for him, and for the rest of us.

37

You're not going to run out of ideas.

We all have that one Great Idea that we're going to do someday, when we're ready—but we hang onto it like it's a bottle of really good wine that we're going to bring out for the proper occasion. And we keep holding onto it, waiting. What if the timing's not right? What if we use it for the wrong situation? Or share it with the wrong people?

A creative idea is not like the last remaining bottle of 1976 Whatever Wine—you can use it, and it isn't necessarily gone forever (like the bottle of wine is). And using it can clear out space for another idea to form.

Don't worry about having enough time for all of your great ideas, because you'll never have enough time. You'll make time for the right ones. As you come up with more ideas, your bad ones will get moved to the bottom of your list and eventually forgotten. Again, don't worry about them. You're not going to run out of ideas. Listen to what Maya Angelou said in a 1982 interview with *Bell Telephone Magazine*:

"You can't use up creativity. The more you use, the more you have."

38

Eventually, you'll have to let it go.

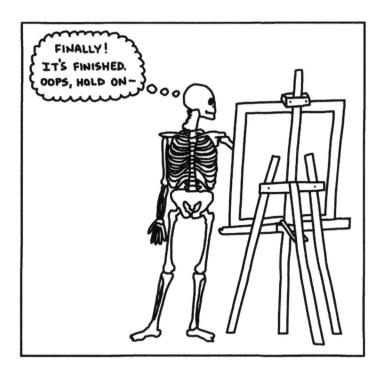

Whatever your creative project is, it's important to realize that it's not a Thanksgiving turkey—a little button isn't going to pop out when it's officially "done."

You can work on a book the rest of your life and never be happy with it, and almost every photo you ever take will have room for improvement somewhere. Leonardo da Vinci famously said, "Art is never finished, only abandoned."

The question you have to ask yourself is not if it's perfect; the question is whether it's ready. Does it say what you want it to say, the best you can say it at this point in your life? When it's ready, you can put it out there.

Don't try to helicopter parent your art. The best you can do is aim it, and hope it shoots somewhere close to where you wanted it to go.

One more famous saying, from the wall at a media company's headquarters circa 2012: "Done is better than perfect." Obviously, you want your thing to be as close to perfect as possible, but keep your focus on getting it done, not endlessly worrying about it not being good enough. Try hard, make progress, and finish it.

39

Spending time working on art is "being creative"—even if you make zero progress.

Everyone who's ever made anything has been there—you plant yourself in front of the keyboard, or easel, or sketchpad, determined to finally get something down, today. And then, an hour or two later, you have ... nothing accomplished. Not a single new paragraph, or a completed drawing, or any new paint on the canvas.

What a waste of time, you say to yourself. But was it really?

Did you explore a dead end, so at least you can cross that option off your list of possibilities? Did you try five different variations of the drawing idea you had, and realized you didn't like any of them? Did you finally research that thing you were going to have the protagonist of your novel do in Chapter 9, if it was actually scientifically possible? Congratulations, that's being creative.

Think about it this way: When a football (soccer) player has a breakaway, running the length of the pitch to score, they're running as fast they can, moving the ball in front of them. Are they kicking, or even tapping, the ball, with their foot every single step? No they are not. You're the player, that ball is your art. Some days you kick it and you can feel your effort turning into progress, and some days you're just running next to it without touching it. But you and your creative work, whatever it is, keep moving forward.

40

Avoiding small clichés will keep your work from being a big cliché.

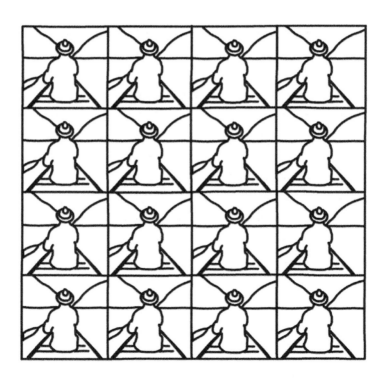

The advice to "avoid clichés" has been drummed into the heads of writers for decades—because if you say things in other writers' words, you'll never develop your own distinct voice. You don't write that your character was driving "like a bat out of hell" and "passing cars like they were standing still" and use phrases that have been spoken millions of times; you come up with you own language to describe the scene.

The same advice is useful in photography, filmmaking, songwriting, and any other creative pursuit. For a few years on social media, you might have seen a very similar photo pop up in your feed over and over again: a paddler on the front seat of a canoe, wearing a red-and-black flannel shirt and maybe a fedora too, their back to the camera as the photographer shoots from the back seat, on a turquoise lake with mountains in the background. There's nothing wrong with all of those photos—they're all really aesthetic, and definitely make me want to be sitting in that canoe on that mountain lake.

And, for sure, when making things for Instagram or other social media, the goal may be to produce something that you know will get engagement, and maybe therefore hopefully sell products, hence the tried-and-true mountain lake canoe shot. But when you're making a piece of art, if your goal is to express yourself, it's a good idea to ask yourself if what you're making is truly your voice.

41

Inhaling creative work can help you exhale creative work.

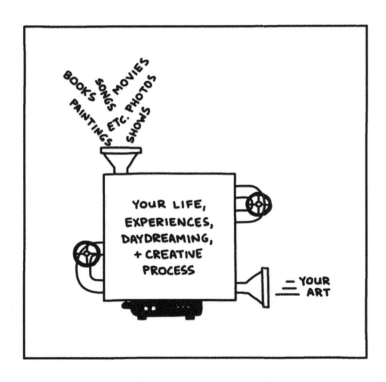

This is quite likely not news to you: Lots of people make art because they love art. We've all heard of filmmakers who grew up watching classic movies, writers who read hundreds of books before they wrote their own, painters who saw a famous painting in a museum or in a book. You're probably the same, in that you love to take in creative works, and think about making your own sometime. The good news is that if you're a fan of art, it's a lot easier to try making art yourself than, say, being a fan of a pro football team and trying to play for them.

Also good news: you can go on being a fan and a being a creative your entire life, and those two things hopefully feed each other. Many successful creatives have talked about this, like Matthew Inman, the artist behind *The Oatmeal*, who wrote in a comic in 2016: "A friend once told me creativity is like breathing. When you make stuff, you're exhaling." Inman explains that he spends a lot of time "inhaling," consuming creative work from diverse sources (not just other cartoonists).

Or Nas, who rapped in "The World Is Yours": "I sip the Dom P, watching *Gandhi* 'til I'm charged/Then writing in my book of rhymes, all the words past the margin". Hunter S. Thompson, who was not religious, used to read the Bible while writing, because he loved the language (and also because he often found himself desperate to meet a deadline in a hotel room with his typewriter and no other books besides the Bible placed in a drawer by the Gideons).

It can be a blessing and a curse to be able to go to art shows, film festivals, and bookstores and libraries and find inspiration for your personal work. Maybe you'll even feel like you're working, analyzing a certain piece for hints, or what you might do differently. Maybe you'll stay up late afterward and work on your thing.

But it's also easy to excuse binge-watching TV shows late into the night, rationalizing that you're "doing research," or "looking for some inspiration," and then realizing you have no time left to make something. So remember to exhale.

42

Creative fulfillment does not equal fame (and vice versa).

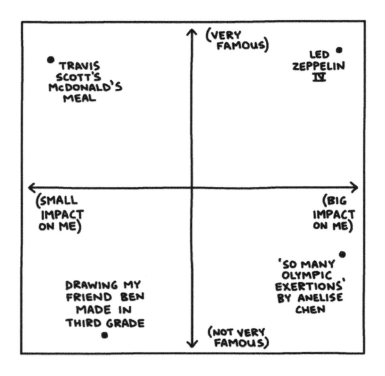

(VERY FAMOUS)

● TRAVIS SCOTT'S McDONALD'S MEAL

LED ● ZEPPELIN IV

←(SMALL IMPACT ON ME)

(BIG IMPACT ON ME)

● 'SO MANY OLYMPIC EXERTIONS' BY ANELISE CHEN

DRAWING MY FRIEND BEN MADE IN THIRD GRADE ●

(NOT VERY FAMOUS)

Sometimes, making art comes with the side effect of becoming famous, but not that often. Sure, lots of the authors, actors, and musicians we can name off the top of our heads are famous, but they make up a tiny percentage of the overall population of people making art, and having fun doing it. If your number-one motivation to make art is to become famous, it might be more efficient to skip the art part and pursue an on-screen role in a reality TV show.

Dave Grohl shared some passionate advice on musicianship in an interview with *Sky Magazine*:

"When I think about kids watching a TV show like *American Idol* or *The Voice*, then they think, 'Oh, OK, that's how you become a musician, you stand in line for eight fucking hours with 800 people at a convention center and then you sing your heart out for someone and then they tell you it's not fucking good enough.' Can you imagine? It's destroying the next generation of musicians. Musicians should go to a yard sale and buy an old fucking drum set and get in their garage and just suck. And get their friends to come in and they'll suck, too. And then they'll fucking start playing and they'll have the best time they've ever had in their lives and then all of a sudden they'll become Nirvana. Because that's exactly what happened with Nirvana. Just a bunch of guys that had some shitty old instruments and they got together and started playing some noisy-ass shit, and they became the biggest band in the world."

43

You're not too busy.

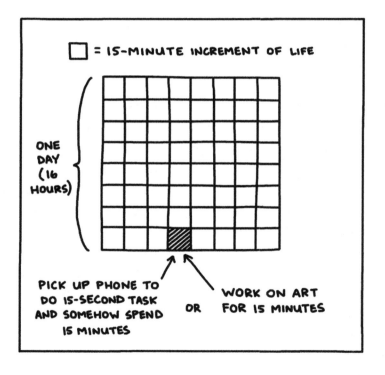

□ = 15-MINUTE INCREMENT OF LIFE

ONE DAY (16 HOURS)

PICK UP PHONE TO DO 15-SECOND TASK AND SOMEHOW SPEND 15 MINUTES

OR

WORK ON ART FOR 15 MINUTES

Yes, you're busy. I understand, because I'm busy too. We're all busy. I'm in no position to judge the way anyone else lives their life, but I am in a good position to judge the way I live mine.

Even during the busiest weeks of my life, when I feel like I haven't had any time in which I was free to sit down and create things, I somehow—according to this app on my phone that tells me exactly how much time I've spent staring at it each day—"make time" to look at it and do the Finger-Tap Dance of Aimlessness for upwards of two hours each day. Sure, I "use my phone for work," and to check the weather, and some other legitimate things, but my gut is that most of that Screen Time is fairly inexcusable.

Now, I'm not some sort of productivity guru, with a dialed-in morning routine, outsourcing and delegating administrative tasks so I can spend the maximum amount of time creating.

But: I do think I have 15 minutes every day that I could spend on Making Something Creative. It's not much, but it's enough to kick a metaphorical ball a little ways down the field—edit a paragraph, re-work a title, draw a sketch of something, scrawl some notes for a future project, or write a goofy poem. And one place I could take that 15 minutes from is my Screen Time. My phone is just one example—there are many other things I spend time on that are much less fulfilling than creativity (ex. Did I just watch a 2 ½-minute video of dogs getting on a doggie daycare bus? Did I just spend four minutes reading a story about a celebrity I'd never heard of before I read the headline? Why do I have four browser tabs open for sneaker shopping, when I have plenty of shoes?).

If I choose to dedicate that 15 minutes to a creative thing, at the end of the day, I'm happier. It just works for me. I'm guessing it might work for you too.

44

Somebody is doing it.

CALENDAR

FEATURING PHOTOS OF THE

GRAND CANYON

THAT ARE WAY BETTER THAN

THE PHOTOS I TOOK

WHEN I VISITED THE GRAND CANYON

Ever shown someone some of your vacation photos of a beautiful place you went and heard yourself saying, "Photos don't do it justice"? I certainly have.

But I've also been lucky enough to go to a few incredible places with a friend who's a professional photographer. Sometimes I've had just an iPhone to take photos with, or sometimes I have my own camera and lenses. And when my friend and I get back and see our finished photos, you know what? Photos did do the place justice. Just not my photos.

You've no doubt heard some version of the saying, "Those who say it can't be done are usually interrupted by others doing it." I personally have had this happen many times in conversations with friends, pretty much like this:

Me: A [something that sounds impossible because of my preconceptions about art, time, money, logistics, whatever]—is that even possible?

Friend: Well, [such-and-such person you've never heard of] is doing it on [YouTube, TikTok, Instagram, etc.], so I guess it is.

There are things that are impossible, for sure (playing in the NBA is probably out for me, at this point). And there are things that are possible for other people because they have more resources or connections than I do, or more spare time. But making lists of the reasons other people have it easier than me isn't the point. The point is: Whatever the thing was, it wasn't impossible.

45

Things are going to take longer than you thought they would.

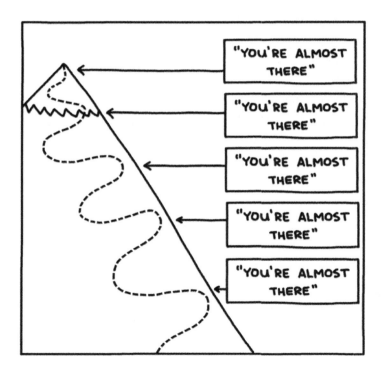

This applies to almost everything, including:

- How long it will take to (finally) start making your art thing

- How long it will take to feel like you've made some progress on it

- How long it will take to get halfway done

- How long cleaning up a single minor detail will take

- How long it will take to finish it (the first time)

- How long it will take you to feel like it's done (because you'll go back and keep messing with it)

- How long it will take for people to "discover" your work

- How long it will take until you feel like you've achieved a bit of something that feels like success

What you may have found doesn't take long:

- A month or a year of your life, passing by

46

You don't have to "stay in your lane."

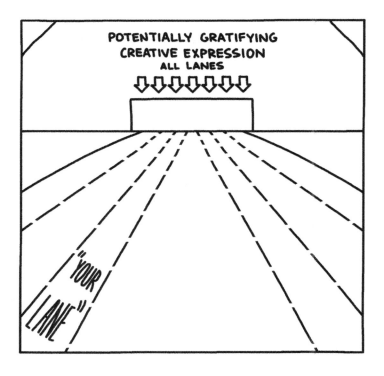

Maybe you've heard something like these words coming out of your mouth:

"I'd love to _____, but I'm really more of a _____ person."

As in "I'd love to write a script for a short film, but I am more of a visual person." Or,

"... but I don't know how to operate a camera."

"... but I've never taken a writing class."

"... but pottery just seems so hard."

"... but somebody told me you need to start playing a musical instrument in your teens or you'll never be any good."

But you don't have to do one thing, or "stay in your lane"—especially if that lane starts to feel like a rut. You can follow what interests you, and dip in and out of things. One example, among many, of an artist who did exactly that:

You've probably heard the song "Hallelujah," one of the most-covered songs ever written. Maybe you heard it in the movie *Shrek*, which was John Cale's cover of it. Or Jeff Buckley's cover of John Cale's version. Or Justin Timberlake's, or Rufus Wainwright's, or Brandi Carlile's, or Regina Spektor's, or Willie Nelson's, or any of the other dozens of versions out there.

Well, that song exists because Leonard Cohen wrote and recorded it in 1984 for his non-hit album *Various Positions*. And Cohen wrote and recorded it because he had been a professional musician since 1967—after he'd tried making a living as a poet and novelist. His books of poetry and fiction did OK, but not as well as he'd hoped, and in 1966, at age 33, he told a friend, "I decided I'm going to be a songwriter. I want to write songs." So he did.

His music career went on for almost five decades, spanning 15 albums, and he was inducted into the Rock 'n' Roll Hall of Fame. He published a couple more books of poetry too, but most people remember his music.

47

Sometimes, you just have to bunt.

CAN YOU POTENTIALLY SCORE A RUN?		
EVENT	YES	NO
YOU GET A BASE HIT	✓	
YOU GET A HOME RUN	✓	
YOU GET A BASE ON BALLS	✓	
YOU GET HIT BY A PITCH	✓	
YOU BUNT	✓	
YOU RUN TO FIRST BASE AFTER A PASSED BALL ON STRIKE 3	✓	
YOU ARE NOT IN THE GAME BECAUSE YOU DECIDED TO NOT PLAY TODAY		✓

If you've ever stepped up to your canvas, or taken out your camera, or opened your laptop, and felt utterly paralyzed by the feeling that you absolutely need to produce your best work, right now, you are far from alone. We all put pressure on ourselves, even if we're not trying to record a follow-up to our Grammy-winning album.

Let me help you with a baseball metaphor: You do not need to hit a home run every day. You just need to get on base. This works in art, just like it does in baseball.

In a famous scene from the baseball movie *Moneyball*, Oakland Athletics general manager Billy Beane is sitting in a meeting room full of the team's scouts, and arguing for the inclusion of several non-top-tier players on next season's roster. Beane has recently become convinced by Peter Brand, a Yale economics graduate, that baseball teams have been evaluating players all wrong—they don't need to focus on a player's batting average and home runs, but simply how often the player gets on base.

Billy Beane says the team should look at a player named Scott Hatteberg, and the room full of scouts is shocked, since Hatteberg allegedly can't throw, can't hit, and has non-repairable nerve damage in his arm. Beane concedes all of that, but points out that Hatteberg gets on base.

Rocco: Alright, so he walks a lot.

Billy Beane: He gets on base a lot, Rocco. Do I care if it's a walk or a hit? Pete?

Pete: You do not.

Take the pressure off yourself when you work on your thing. You don't have to swing for the fences every time. You just have to get on base.

48

You don't have to share it with people, or make money off of it, or even keep it.

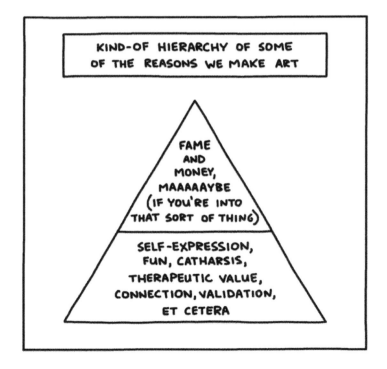

KIND-OF HIERARCHY OF SOME
OF THE REASONS WE MAKE ART

FAME
AND
MONEY,
MAAAAAYBE
(IF YOU'RE INTO
THAT SORT OF THING)

SELF-EXPRESSION,
FUN, CATHARSIS,
THERAPEUTIC VALUE,
CONNECTION, VALIDATION,
ET CETERA

Sure, it would be wonderful to get rich (not that rich, just a little bit), and maybe famous (OK, not really famous, but just a little bit famous), and receive validation (and maybe even some admiration) from people because you made a book or a movie or a song or a painting that resonated with your fellow human beings. And we, at least in the United States, seem to conflate artistic success with financial success and fame a lot of the time.

But you can express yourself by making things, and you can sell five of them, or not sell them at all. You can give them away. You can make things and share them with ten people, or zero people. You can make a drawing and when you're finished, you can tear it into a hundred pieces and throw them in the trash.

There are no rules for making art, and there are certainly no rules for what to do with it when it's completed. People have a billion different reasons for making things, and all of them are generally valid (except, you could argue, making it to hurt other people, but that's a different conversation).

49

People are going to bring their own stuff to your art.

You might expect that your favorite book of all time would have a very high rating on Goodreads. Especially if it was written by a renowned author who won the Nobel Prize in Literature, and it's by far their most famous book. You might think, out of five possible stars on Goodreads, it would have an average pretty close to five stars, or at least four-point-seven something? Well, in the overwhelming majority of cases, you'd be wrong. Your favorite book, which you might think is the best book ever written, probably has an average Goodreads rating around 3.8 to 4.2. Why? Because a lot of people don't think your favorite book is as great as you do. Why?

Well, you can read some of the reviews, which might leave you scratching your head a little bit. Why would someone be mad that there was so much talk about birds, when the cover blurb says the book is about ... birds? Why would a reader give a book a bad review because it reminded them of their uncle, who they hated? Why would someone give a nonfiction book a one-star review because it was not fiction?

People bring all kinds of life experiences and views to art when they experience it, and if your work gets out there to enough people, you might encounter someone's opinion that might leave you asking, "Why in the world would they think that?"

Sometimes they have a point, and sometimes you might just have to brush it off and say, "It's not me, it's you."

50

Being creative as an adult is a survival story.

Every one of us, at one point when we were very young, made a drawing and we had no reservations about whether it was any good or not. We may not remember it, but we did. And then we grew up, gradually or all at once, over several years, and we realized other people could have opinions about us.

After that, we very likely stopped doing things we thought other people might see as not very good. We stopped making bad drawings, nonsensical song lyrics, stories that didn't make any sense to anyone but our parents (or nearby doll or teddy bear), and wearing a bedsheet as a cape to feel like our favorite superhero.

Continuing to create as an adult is a survival story, and the survivor is the little kid you used to be, who didn't worry about being "bad" at drawing, or playing the kazoo, or writing poems. Losing our innocence is unavoidable in life, but the loss of our ability to create, or to just play, is something we can regain at any age.

So have some fun, don't worry about the end result, and make some stuff, even if some of it isn't that good. You won't regret it.

For more:

Brendan Leonard's writing, illustrations, books, short films, and weekly newsletter can be found on his website, Semi-Rad.com, or on social media @semi_rad.

Printed in Great Britain
by Amazon